E hoʻolono i ka mele, he mel

carries a mele, a song of old Hawaiʻi, throughout Nuʻuanu Valley.

Memories of majesty
linger at Hānaiakamalama.

Aia i uka o Nuʻuanu,
ma Hānaiakamalama.

Memories of majesty
linger at Hānaiakamalama.

Aia i uka o Nuʻuanu,
ma Hānaiakamalama.

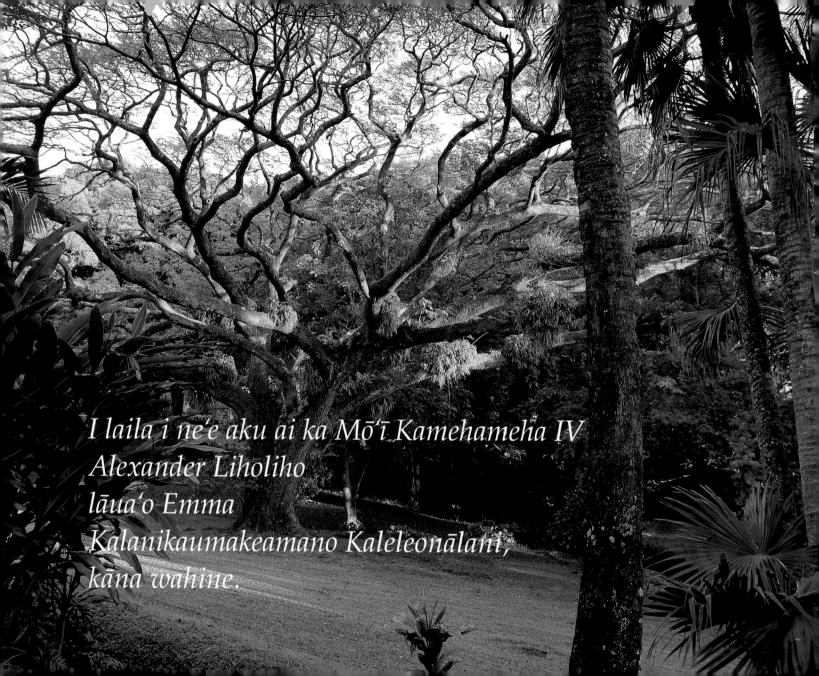

I laila i neʻe aku ai ka Mōʻī Kamehameha IV
Alexander Liholiho
lāuaʻo Emma
Kalanikaumakeamano Kaleleonālani,
kāna wahine.

Amidst ʻōhai trees and lokelani, *heavenly roses, Queen Emma and King Kamehameha IV retreated from the heat of Honolulu in 1856.*

He home hoʻokipa me nā malihini
He home aloha
He home nani
He home hoʻopiha me nā mea kamaʻāina aloha
a me nā mea mai nā ʻāina ʻē.

The newlywed couple soon discovered
a haven at Hānaiakamalama . . .

. . . a home where gracious hospitality, music, refined conversation, and the harmony of many cultures reigned.

*Aia nā mea waiwai o Hawai'i
i loko o nā lumi,
'o ia ho'i . . .*

*. . . nā kāhili i haku ʻia e nā manu kamaʻāina
o Hawaiʻi, a me nā puke me nā makana mai nā aliʻi
mai nā ʻāina Palani, Pelekane, ʻInia, Pākē, a me Kahiki.*

*Crowned
by kāhili
made from
the feathers
of native birds,
the rooms
were graced
with books
and treasures
from monarchs
near and far . . .*

. . . the kings and
queens of France
and England,
a maharajah of
India, the emperor
of China, the
princess of Tahiti,
and sacred
artifacts inherited
from the royal
lineage of ali'i.

*Beloved and
benevolent,
the royal
couple ruled
the Islands
with pomp
and pageantry,*
na'auao,
*wisdom,
and* aloha
'āina, *love
of the land.*

Noho
aupuni
kēia mau
ali'i me ka
ha'aha'a,
ka mana'o'i'o,
ka na'auao,
a me ke aloha,
ke aloha
nui no ka
'āina a me
nā po'e apau.

A twenty-one gun salute
heralded great news in 1858.
His Royal Highness the Prince
of Hawai'i and godson
of Queen Victoria was born.

Ua hānau 'ia mai ke ali'i
Albert Edward
Kauikeaouli Leiopapa
Ā Kamehameha.

Cradled in adoration, the crown prince, noble heir of the Kamehameha dynasty, had but one wish . . .

*'O ia nō Ka Haku O Hawai'i,
ke keiki aloha ā ka Mō'ī Kamehameha IV
a me Emma.*

. . . to become a fireman!
Trumpets sounded as he
paraded as an honorary member
of Fire Company No. 4.

'O Queen Victoria
kona makuahine papakema.

Aloha ʻia mai keia keiki aliʻi
hiwahiwa e nā ʻano poʻe likeʻole.

Sadly and suddenly, the precious
young sovereign died at age four.
Overnight a lilting lullaby became
a nation's lament, Auwē nōhoʻi ē.

A bereaved Queen Emma
composed a poem to mourn the loss
of a son and, in a year's time, the death
of a husband, the end of an era.

'Eha ka na'au a kaumaha loa
ka Mō'īwahine Emma i ka hala 'ana
o kana keiki, a ma hope iho, kana kāne.

Hu'ihu'i ka 'āina me ke kanikau no lāua. Auwē nōho'i ē!

A chill sweeps the valley . . .

E ola mau ka mana o nā aliʻi ma Hānaiakamalama
eō mai e nā pua o Hawaiʻi nei!

. . . and a whisper
of a chant
evokes the
past.

Serenaded
by tradition
and heritage,
Hānaiakamalama
is surrounded
by a melody
of memories
of majesty
for all the sons
and daughters
of Hawai'i nei.

Ma keia home
ho'opiha no
nā malihini,
he home aloha,
he home nani,
he home ho'opiha
me nā mea
kama'āina
aloha a me
nā mea mai
nā 'āina 'ē.

Serenaded
by tradition
and heritage,
Hānaiakamalama
is surrounded
by a melody
of memories
of majesty
for all the sons
and daughters
of Hawai'i nei.

Ma keia home
ho'opila no
nā malihini,
he home aloha,
he home nani,
he home ho'opila
me nā mea
kama'āina
aloha a me
nā mea mai
nā 'āina 'ē.

Memories of Majesty at Hānaiakamalama

Text by Susan Mau Soong

Photography by Linny Morris Cunningham

Design by Steve Shrader

The publication of this book was made possible through the generous gifts of Brendan and Roy Mesker; Alexander & Baldwin, Inc.; The Atherton Family Foundation and an anonymous donor.

Published by
Daughters of Hawaii
2913 Pali Highway
Honolulu, Hawai'i 96817

Publications committee:
Leilani Adams Maguire, chairman
Christiane Bryan Bintliff
Frances Kay Brossy
Ellin White Burkland
Evanita Sumner Midkiff
Jeanne Hoyt Shedd
Shannon Heath Wilson

With assistance from Virginia Dominis Koch, collections chairman; Mildred Hedemann Nolan, historian; Leiana Long Woodside, curator; Mealani Evensen; Lauren Hokulani Apiki and Dr. Rhoda Hackler

Printed in Hong Kong

     ISBN 0-938851-10-1

The Photographs

Note: All starred items (*) are part of the permanent collection of the Daughters of Hawaii at Queen Emma Summer Palace.

Front cover: Bisque bust of Queen Emma*; Queen Emma Summer Palace in the evening.

Inside front cover & page 1: Nu'uanu Valley.

Page 2: Gold double-framed daguerreotype of Alexander Liholiho and Emma Na'ea Rooke*.

Page 5: The veranda at Queen Emma Summer Palace, including koa furniture*.

Page 6: Monkeypod tree on the grounds of Queen Emma Summer Palace.

Page 7: Roses from Queen Emma's garden.

Pages 8 & 9: Queen Emma's wedding dress*.

Page 9: One of a pair of beds made for King Kamehameha IV by Wilhelm Fischer*, with Hawaiian quilt*.

Page 10: Parlor of Queen Emma Summer Palace, showing red tufted chenille upholstered chair *; footstool (on loan from the Honolulu Academy of Arts); mirror and table*; ecru and navy Chinese porcelain vase with carved ivory handles*; Emil Ascher-berg baby grand piano, purchased by Queen Emma in Dresden, Germany*; portrait above the piano of Alapa'i, wife of Queen Emma's uncle, John Young II*; koa table and chairs*; Canton bowl*.

Page 11: see page 12.

Page 12: Three portraits (L to R) Queen Victoria by F. Winterhalter*, Queen Emma*, and Prince Albert Edward, consort to Queen Victoria, by F. Winterhalter*; original piano that Queen Emma learned to play on, manufactured by Collard & Collard in London, England*; bisque bust of Queen Emma*; kāhili*; red velvet recliner of King Kamehameha IV's (indefinite loan from the Honolulu Academy of Arts); in the background, koa sideboard of Queen Emma's*.

Page 13: Various hand-held kāhili*.

Page 14: Gold framed mirror*; upholstered chair*; Queen Emma's lorgnette*; table with brown marble top*; *Campbell's Poetical Works*; amethyst bracelet that the Duke of Edinburgh brought to Hawai'i as a gift to Queen Emma*; gold bud vase ring of Queen Emma's*; *Montgomery's Poetical Works*; brown leather book, marked "ER" with a crown*; silver teapot and creamer inscribed "Hānaiaka-malama" (part of a five-piece set)*; 24-karat gold-plated silver flatware, engraved "ER", (part of 37-piece set)*.

Page 15: Edinburgh Room, Queen Emma Summer Palace, including two kāhili*, portraits (L to R) of King Kamehameha II (Liholiho)*, Queen Kamamalu*, Queen Kalama*, King Kamehameha III (Kauikeaouli)*; in the center is the gold-framed mirror and accompanying marble-top table*; crystal chandelier *; three chairs and settee, believed to have been Kamehameha V's*; large round koa table *; calabash*; two small round tables*; gold clock*.

Page 16: Tiger claw necklace, a gift to Queen Emma upon the occasion of her marriage, from an Indian maharajah*.

Page 17: China cabinet, made in Berlin, partly of koa wood, received as a wedding gift by Queen Emma from Queen Victoria and Prince Albert Edward of England *; Copeland china, within, received as a gift by Queen Emma from Queen Victoria*.

Page 18: (Above) pūniu (coconut-shell bowl) on silver stand, engraved "Gift of Ninito Sumner of Tahiti 1879"*. (Below) porcelain bathtub presented to Prince Albert of Hawai'i by the emperor of China*.